"9Marks, as a ministry, has taken ba~~s~~ the hands of pastors. Bobby, by way delivered it to the person in the pew. ~~I am unaware of any other tool that so thoroughly~~ and practically helps Christians understand God's plan for the local church. I can't wait to use these studies in my own congregation."

Jeramie Rinne, Senior Pastor, South Shore Baptist Church, Hingham, Massachusetts

"Bobby Jamieson has done local church pastors an incredible service by writing these study guides. Clear, biblical, and practical, they introduce the biblical basis for a healthy church. But more importantly, they challenge and equip church members to be part of the process of improving their own church's health. The studies work for individual, small group, and larger group settings. I have used them for the last year at my own church and appreciate how easy they are to adapt to my own setting. I don't know of anything else like them. Highly recommended!"

Michael Lawrence, Senior Pastor, Hinson Baptist Church, *Biblical Theology in the Life of the Church*

"This is a Bible study that is actually rooted in the Bible and involves actual study. In the 9Marks Healthy Church Study Guides series a new standard has been set for personal theological discovery and corresponding personal application. Rich exposition, compelling questions, and clear syntheses combine to give a guided tour of ecclesiology—the theology of the church. I know of no better curriculum for generating understanding of and involvement in the church than this. It will be a welcome resource in our church for years to come."

Rick Holland, Senior Pastor, Mission Road Bible Church, Prairie Village, Kansas

"In America today we have the largest churches in the history of our nation, but the least amount of impact for Christ's kingdom. Slick marketing and finely polished vision statements are a foundation of sand. The 9Marks Healthy Church Study Guides series is a refreshing departure from church-growth materials, towards an in-depth study of God's Word that will equip God's people with his vision for his Church. These study guides will lead local congregations to abandon secular methodologies for church growth and instead rely on Christ's principles for developing healthy, God-honoring assemblies."

Carl J. Broggi, Senior Pastor, Community Bible Church, Beaufort, South Carolina; President, Search the Scriptures Radio Ministry

"Anyone who loves Jesus will love what Jesus loves. The Bible clearly teaches that Jesus loves the church. He knows about and cares for individual churches and wants them to be spiritually healthy and vibrant. Not only has Jesus laid down his life for the church but he has also given many instructions in his Word regarding how churches are to live and function in the world. This series of Bible studies by 9Marks shows how Scripture teaches these things. Any Christian who works through this curriculum, preferably with other believers, will be helped to see in fresh ways the wisdom, love, and power of God in establishing the church on earth. These studies are biblical, practical, and accessible. I highly recommend this curriculum as a useful tool that will help any church embrace its calling to display the glory of God to a watching world."

Thomas Ascol, Senior Pastor, Grace Baptist Church of Cape Coral, Florida; Executive Director, Founders Ministries

9MARKS HEALTHY CHURCH STUDY GUIDES

Built upon the Rock: The Church

Hearing God's Word: Expositional Preaching

The Whole Truth about God: Biblical Theology

God's Good News: The Gospel

Real Change: Conversion

Reaching the Lost: Evangelism

Committing to One Another: Church Membership

Guarding One Another: Church Discipline

Growing One Another: Discipleship in the Church

Leading One Another: Church Leadership

GROWING ONE ANOTHER: DISCIPLESHIP IN THE CHURCH

Bobby Jamieson
Mark Dever, General Editor
Jonathan Leeman, Managing Editor

HEALTHY CHURCH STUDY GUIDES

:: CROSSWAY®

WHEATON, ILLINOIS

Crossway is a publishing ministry of Good News Publishers.

VP		26	25	24	23	22	21	20	19
17	16	15	14	13	12	11	10	9	8

CONTENTS

Introduction   7

An Important Mark of a Healthy Church:
Biblical Discpleship and Growth, *by Mark Dever*   11

WEEK 1
The Need for Discipleship   15

WEEK 2
The Definition of Discipleship   19

WEEK 3
The Motivations of Discipleship   23

WEEK 4
The Means of Discipleship: Following Godly Examples   27

WEEK 5
The Means of Discipleship: Teaching One Another   31

WEEK 6
The Enemy of Discipleship: Indwelling Sin   35

WEEK 7
The End of Discipleship   39

Teacher's Notes   43

INTRODUCTION

What does the local church mean to you?

Maybe you love your church. You love the people. You love the preaching, the singing. You can't wait to show up on Sunday, and you cherish fellowship with other church members throughout the week.

Maybe the church is just a place you show up to a couple times a month. You sneak in late, duck out early.

We at 9Marks are convinced that the local church is God's plan for displaying his glory to the nations. And we want to help you catch and live out that vision, together with your whole church.

The 9Marks Healthy Church Study Guides are a series of six- or seven-week studies on each of the "nine marks of a healthy church" plus one introductory study. These nine marks are the core convictions of our ministry. To provide a quick introduction to them, we've included a chapter from Mark Dever's book *What Is a Healthy Church?* with each study. We don't claim that these nine marks are the most important things about the church or the only important things about the church. But we do believe that they are biblical and therefore are helpful for churches.

So, in these studies, we're going to work through the biblical foundations and practical applications of each one. The ten studies are:

- *Built upon the Rock: The Church* (the introductory study)
- *Hearing God's Word: Expositional Preaching*
- *The Whole Truth about God: Biblical Theology*
- *God's Good News: The Gospel*
- *Real Change: Conversion*
- *Reaching the Lost: Evangelism*
- *Committing to One Another: Church Membership*

- *Guarding One Another: Church Discipline*
- *Growing One Another: Discipleship in the Church*
- *Leading One Another: Church Leadership*

Each session of these studies takes a close look at one or more passages of Scripture and considers how it applies to the life of the whole church. So, we hope that these studies are equally appropriate for Sunday school, small groups, and other contexts where a group of anywhere from two to two-hundred people can come together and discuss God's Word.

These studies are mainly driven by observation, interpretation, and application questions, so get ready to speak up! We also hope that these studies provide opportunities for people to reflect together on their experiences in the church, whatever those experiences may be.

When Jesus called Peter and Andrew to leave their fishing gear and follow him, he called them to a whole new life. And when Jesus calls each of us to be his disciple, he calls us to a whole new life.

Following Jesus means listening to him, watching him, and following in his footsteps. It means hating what Jesus hates and loving what Jesus loves.

It also means helping others to do the same. After his resurrection Jesus commanded his disciples to go and make more disciples, teaching them to obey everything Jesus commanded.

And, as we will see throughout this study, God intends the local church to be the main context for disciple making. God established the church to affirm disciples, oversee disciples, and raise up more disciples.

All of this is possible because of what Jesus has already done for us. He has paid the penalty for our sins. He has reconciled us to God. Through our union with his death and resurrection, we have a new life, a new self. Before, we were rebels. Now, we're glad subjects of the King of kings, and we love to do what he commands.

This study, then, focuses on growing in Christ and helping others do the same—in local churches. We'll consider:

- The need for discipleship
- The definition of discipleship
- The motivations of discipleship
- The means of discipleship
- The enemy of discipleship
- The end of discipleship

Are you striving to grow in Christ and to help others do the same? Our prayer is that this study will help you to do that more and more faithfully.

-

AN IMPORTANT MARK OF A HEALTHY CHURCH: BIBLICAL DISCIPLESHIP AND GROWTH

BY MARK DEVER

(Originally published as chapter 12 of What Is a Healthy Church?*)*

An important mark of a healthy church is a pervasive concern for church growth as growth is prescribed in the Bible. That means growing members, not just numbers.

Some today think that a person can be a "baby Christian" for a whole lifetime. Growth is treated as an optional extra for zealous disciples. But growth is a sign of life. If a tree is alive, it grows. If an animal is alive, it grows. Being alive means growing, and growing means increasing and advancing, at least until death intercedes.

Paul hoped the Corinthians would grow in their faith (2 Cor. 10:15), and that the Ephesians would "grow up into him who is the Head, that is, Christ" (Eph. 4:15 NIV; cf. Col. 1:10; 2 Thess. 1:3). Peter exhorted his readers, "Like newborn babies, crave pure spiritual milk, so that by it you may grow up in your salvation" (1 Peter 2:2 NIV).

It is tempting for pastors and even some members to reduce their churches to manageable statistics of attendance, baptisms, giving, and membership. This kind of growth is tangible. Yet such statistics fall far short of the true growth that the New Testament authors describe and that God desires.

GROWTH IN HOLINESS

How do we know when Christians are growing in grace? We don't ultimately know from the fact that they're excited, use lots of religious language, or have a growing knowledge of Scripture. Just because they exhibit an increased love for the church or display confidence in their own faith isn't determinative either. We can't even be sure Christians are growing because they appear to have an outward zeal for God. All these may be evidences of true Christian growth. At the same time, one of the most important and commonly overlooked signs of growth that must be observed is increasing holiness rooted in Christian self-denial (see James 2:20–24; 2 Pet. 1:5–11). The church should be marked by a vital concern for this kind of increasing godliness in the lives of its members.

Neglecting holiness, like neglecting church discipline, results in hard-to-grow disciples. In churches where unholy behavior goes unchecked, disciples become confused and unclear about the life that is honoring to Christ. It's like a garden where the weeds are never pulled or good things are never planted.

WHAT GROWTH DOES AND DOESN'T LOOK LIKE

The church has an obligation to be God's means of growing people in grace. Mature, holiness-seeking influences in a covenant community of believers can be tools in God's hand for growing his people. As God's people are built up and grow together in holiness and self-giving love, they should improve their ability to administer discipline and to encourage discipleship.

When you peer into the life of a church, the growth of its members can show up in all sorts of ways. Here are a few possibilities:

- Growing numbers being called to missions—"I've enjoyed sharing the gospel with my neighbors from South America. I wonder if God is calling me to. . . . "
- Older members getting a fresh sense of their responsibility in evangelism and in discipling younger members—"Why don't you come over for dinner?"

- Younger members attending the funerals of older members out of love—"As a single man in my twenties, it was so good to be taken in by Mr. and Mrs. . . . . "
- Increased praying in the church and more prayers centered on evangelism and ministry opportunities—"I'm starting an evangelistic Bible study at work and I'm a little nervous. Would the church pray that. . . . "
- More members sharing the gospel with outsiders.
- Less reliance among members on the church's programs and more spontaneous ministry activities arising from members—"Pastor, what would you think if Sally and I organized a Christmas tea for the ladies in the church as an evangelistic opportunity?"
- Informal gatherings among church members characterized by spiritual conversation, including an apparent willingness to confess sin while simultaneously pointing to the cross—"Hey brother, I'm really struggling with. . . . "
- Increased and sacrificial giving—"Honey, how can we cut fifty dollars from our monthly budget in order to support. . . . "
- Increased fruits of the Spirit.
- Members making career sacrifices so that they can serve the church—"Did you hear that Chris turned down a promotion three times so that he could continue devoting himself to being an elder?"
- Husbands leading their wives sacrificially—"Honey, what are several things I can do to make you feel more loved and understood?"
- Wives submitting to their husbands—"Sweetheart, what are some things I can do today that will make your life easier?"
- Parents discipling their children in the faith—"Tonight let's pray for Christian workers in the country of. . . . "
- A corporate willingness to discipline unrepentant and public sin.
- A corporate love for an unrepentant sinner shown in the pursuit of him or her before discipline is enacted—"Please! If you get this message, I would love to hear from you."

These are just a few examples of the kind of church growth for which Christians should pray and work. Will healthy churches grow in size? They often do, because they present an attractive witness to the gospel. But we should not assume they must. Sometimes God has other purposes, such as calling his people to patience. Our focus must remain on faithfulness and true spiritual growth.

And what's the cause of such growth? Expositional Bible preaching. Sound biblical theology. Gospel-centeredness. And a biblical understanding of conversion, evangelism, membership, discipline, and leadership!

But if churches are places where only the pastor's thoughts are taught, where God is questioned more than he is worshiped, where the gospel is diluted and evangelism perverted, where church membership is made meaningless, and a worldly cult of personality is allowed to grow up around the pastor, then one can hardly expect to find a community that is either cohesive or edifying. Such a church will not glorify God.

GOD GLORIFIED BY GROWTH

When we encounter a church composed of members growing in Christlikeness, who gets the glory? God does, because, as Paul said, "God made it grow. So neither he who plants nor he who waters is anything, but only God, who makes things grow" (1 Cor. 3:6b–7 NIV; cf. Col. 2:19).

Likewise, Peter concludes his second letter to a group of early Christians, "Grow in the grace and knowledge of our Lord and Savior Jesus Christ. To him be glory both now and forever! Amen" (2 Pet. 3:18 NIV). We might think that our growth will bring glory to ourselves. But Peter knew better: "Live such good lives among the pagans that, though they accuse you of doing wrong, they may see your good deeds and glorify God on the day he visits us" (1 Pet. 2:12 NIV). Peter obviously remembered Jesus's words: "Let your light shine before others, that they may see your good deeds and [praise you?" No! ". . . And] praise your Father in heaven" (Matt. 5:16 NIV). Working to promote Christian discipleship and growth is another mark of a healthy church.

WEEK 1
THE NEED FOR
DISCIPLESHIP

GETTING STARTED

1. *What was the last experience you had that showed you that you still have a lot to learn, whether at home, at work, in church, or in any other area of life?*

This whole study is going to focus on discipleship. To be a disciple is to be a student, someone who learns from and imitates his teacher. As disciples of Jesus Christ, we are all called to continually learn from him and follow him in every area of life.

Practically speaking, this means that we need to realize that discipleship is a lifelong process. In this life, none of us is a finished product. We all need to continually progress as disciples.

MAIN IDEA

None of us is perfect. We all need to grow as disciples of Christ.

DIGGING IN

In Philippians 3:8–11, Paul exclaims that everything that once caused him to be proud he now considers to have been a waste of time because of the surpassing worth of knowing Christ. He then explains why he has gladly lost all of that and more: it's allowed him to know Christ, to share in his sufferings, and to attain to the resurrection from the dead.

But in case anyone might think that Paul was saying that he had become perfectly mature, Paul continues:

> [12] Not that I have already obtained this or am already perfect, but I press on to make it my own, because Christ Jesus has made me

his own. [13] Brothers, I do not consider that I have made it my own. But one thing I do: forgetting what lies behind and straining forward to what lies ahead, [14] I press on toward the goal for the prize of the upward call of God in Christ Jesus. [15] Let those of us who are mature think this way, and if in anything you think otherwise, God will reveal that also to you. [16] Only let us hold true to what we have attained.

[17] Brothers, join in imitating me, and keep your eyes on those who walk according to the example you have in us. [18] For many, of whom I have often told you and now tell you even with tears, walk as enemies of the cross of Christ. [19] Their end is destruction, their god is their belly, and they glory in their shame, with minds set on earthly things. [20] But our citizenship is in heaven, and from it we await a Savior, the Lord Jesus Christ, [21] who will transform our lowly body to be like his glorious body, by the power that enables him even to subject all things to himself. (Phil. 3:12–21)

1. *What does Paul say that he is not, and that he has not yet done (vv. 12–13)?*

2. *If this is how the apostle Paul viewed himself, what does that say about what our own attitudes toward ourselves should be?*

3. *What reason does Paul give for why he presses on to obtain a deeper knowledge of Christ (v. 12)?*

4. *What does this teach us about the basis and motivation for our growth as Christians?*

5. *What is the one thing that Paul does do (vv. 13–14)?*

6. *What kind of imagery does Paul use in verses 13 and 14? What does it remind you of? What does this teach us about the kind of effort we should spend on growing as Christians?*

7. *Whom does Paul instruct us to imitate in verse 17? (Hint: There are two answers.)*

8. What does this teach us about how we are to grow as Christians?

9. What is the threat Paul mentions to our faithfully following his and others' godly example (vv. 18–19)? Why does this threat make it especially important for us to follow godly examples?

10. List everything Paul says is true of us as Christians in verses 20 to 21. How does each of these things encourage us to persevere in our discipleship?

11. How do you respond when a fellow believer corrects or rebukes you? What does this reveal about how you see yourself?

12. In this study we've seen that all of us need to continually grow as disciples of Jesus Christ, and that we are to do so by seeking out and imitating godly examples. Can you list one or two people who are worth being imitated? What Christlike qualities do you perceive in those individuals that are worth imitating?

13. Paul presents himself as an example to be imitated. A person could do this out of pride, but explain how one could also do this out of humility.

14. Is your life one which younger Christians should imitate? If not, do you work to become that kind of person?

15. What is one practical way you can seek to grow as a disciple of Jesus Christ this week?

WEEK 2
THE DEFINITION OF
DISCIPLESHIP

GETTING STARTED

1. What comes into your mind when you think about "discipleship"? Is it a good thing or a bad thing?

MAIN IDEA

Discipleship means growing as followers of Jesus and helping others to do the same.

DIGGING IN

Throughout the Gospels, Jesus calls people to leave everything and follow him. Read all of the following passages aloud:

[18] While walking by the Sea of Galilee, he saw two brothers, Simon (who is called Peter) and Andrew his brother, casting a net into the sea, for they were fishermen. [19] And he said to them, "Follow me, and I will make you fishers of men." [20] Immediately they left their nets and followed him. (Matt. 4:18–20)

[9] As Jesus passed on from there, he saw a man called Matthew sitting at the tax booth, and he said to him, "Follow me." And he rose and followed him. (Matt. 9:9)

[24] Then Jesus told his disciples, "If anyone would come after me, let him deny himself and take up his cross and follow me. [25] For whoever would save his life will lose it, but whoever loses his life for my sake will find it." (Matt. 16:24–25)

[25] Whoever loves his life loses it, and whoever hates his life in this world will keep it for eternal life. [26] If anyone serves me, he must

follow me; and where I am, there will my servant be also. If anyone
serves me, the Father will honor him. (John 12:25–26)

*1. Based on these passages, what does it mean to follow Jesus? List as many
things as you can think of below.*

*2. Does following Jesus mean that we must leave our jobs or other responsibili-
ties, as Peter, Andrew, and Matthew all did? Explain your answer from Scripture.*

3. According to these passages, is following Jesus easy?

As we considered in our previous study, none of us are perfect.
All of us need to continually grow as followers of Jesus. Although
there is certainly a point at which all of us first believed the gospel
and submitted our lives to Christ, we are not true followers of Jesus
if we simply made a "decision" at some point and our lives haven't
changed at all.

Rather, being Christians—disciples of Jesus—means that we con-
stantly repent of sin, confess it, seek to overcome it, and do all that
we can to grow in likeness to Christ. As Peter tells us, "But grow in the
grace and knowledge of our Lord and Savior Jesus Christ" (2 Pet. 3:18).
To be a follower of Jesus is to be always growing in following Jesus.

Let's consider another passage of Scripture that helps to define
discipleship. At the very end of the book of Matthew, Jesus gives his
eleven disciples the charge which has come to be known as the Great
Commission. He says,

All authority in heaven and on earth has been given to me. [19] Go
therefore and make disciples of all nations, baptizing them in the
name of the Father and of the Son and of the Holy Spirit, [20] teaching
them to observe all that I have commanded you. And behold, I am
with you always, to the end of the age. (Matt. 28:18–20)

*4. What does Jesus say has been given to him (v. 18)? What does that require
of us?*

5. What does Jesus command his disciples to do? How are they to do it (vv. 19–20)?

6. Do you think this passage applies to believers today, or was it only for the eleven disciples? Explain your answer from the text.

7. What encouragement does Jesus give us in this task of making disciples (v. 20)?

8. What are some things that could cause us to be discouraged as we seek to make disciples? How does Jesus's promise to be with us help us during those times?

9. We typically associate this passage with cross-cultural missions, which is certainly something that this passage requires. But is that this passage's only application? What do you think?

As we've seen in this passage, Jesus's followers are to obey all of his commands, which include this command to go and make disciples. This means that all disciples of Jesus are to work to make other disciples of Jesus, first by proclaiming the good news of the gospel to them, and then, for those who respond in faith, teaching them to do everything that Jesus has commanded.

To be a follower of Jesus is to help others grow as followers of Jesus.

10. Do you think about every single area of your life through the lens of being a follower of Jesus? What's one area in your life in which you struggle to follow Jesus?

Here's one practical way for you to follow up on the last question. Do you know a believer who sets a godly example in the area of discipleship you struggle with?

- If so, ask if you can get together with this person and discuss this matter. God means for us to grow through the help of others.
- If not, ask around at church until you find someone who does!

21

11. Have you considered that a normal part of being a follower of Jesus is helping others grow as followers of Jesus? What are some ways this truth should impact:

a) Your daily schedule?
b) How you approach going to church on Sunday?
c) Casual conversations with friends?
d) Other areas of your life?

WEEK 3
THE MOTIVATIONS OF
DISCIPLESHIP

GETTING STARTED
1. *Is there anything in your life that you're required to do, but you consistently struggle to find motivation for? How do you respond? Where do you go to find the motivation you need?*

In this study we're going to consider the motivations of discipleship. Why should we seek to obey God and grow in holiness? What are the right reasons for trying to grow as Christians and helping others do the same?

MAIN IDEA
We should grow as Christians and help others do the same because of who God is, what he has done for us in Christ, and who he has made us in Christ.

DIGGING IN
In Colossians 3, the apostle Paul lays out a vision for growing as disciples of Jesus that is based upon a rich diversity of motivations. He writes,

> [1] If then you have been raised with Christ, seek the things that are above, where Christ is, seated at the right hand of God. [2] Set your minds on things that are above, not on things that are on earth. [3] For you have died, and your life is hidden with Christ in God. [4] When Christ who is your life appears, then you also will appear with him in glory.
> [5] Put to death therefore what is earthly in you: sexual immorality, impurity, passion, evil desire, and covetousness, which is

idolatry. [6] On account of these the wrath of God is coming. [7] In these you too once walked, when you were living in them. [8] But now you must put them all away: anger, wrath, malice, slander, and obscene talk from your mouth. [9] Do not lie to one another, seeing that you have put off the old self with its practices [10] and have put on the new self, which is being renewed in knowledge after the image of its creator. [11] Here there is not Greek and Jew, circumcised and uncircumcised, barbarian, Scythian, slave, free; but Christ is all, and in all.

[12] Put on then, as God's chosen ones, holy and beloved, compassionate hearts, kindness, humility, meekness, and patience, [13] bearing with one another and, if one has a complaint against another, forgiving each other; as the Lord has forgiven you, so you also must forgive. (Col. 3:1–13)

1. What does Paul command us to do in verse 1? On what basis does Paul command us to do this (v. 1)?

2. Paul is saying that although we were spiritually dead, we have now been raised to life with Christ, and now we are seated with Christ in heaven. Does this make you want to grow as a disciple of Jesus? Why or why not?

3. How is this motivation for discipleship different from a "just do it" approach, where we seek to obey God out of a bare sense of obligation?

4. What does Paul command us to do in verse 2? On what grounds does Paul command us to do this (vv. 3–4)?

5. In verse 3, Paul says that, if you're a Christian, you've died. You've died to your old self. You've died to sin. You've died to the power of this world which once held you captive. How does the fact that you've died to sin encourage you to pursue holiness?

6. In verse 4, Paul reminds us that when Christ appears, we will also appear with him in glory.

    a) Think about a difficult task you've completed that had a specific goal in mind, like a race or a project on a deadline. Now imagine if the outcome of that task you're striving for is perfectly sure and will certainly happen. How would that affect your effort in the present?

b) In a similar way, how should the certain hope of being glorified with Christ fuel your efforts to grow in Christ now?

In sum, the first four verses of this passage motivate our growth in godliness by reminding us of our death to sin and new life in Christ (vv. 1–3), and the certain hope of future glory with Christ (v. 4).

7. What does Paul say to "put to death" in verse 5? What does it mean to "put to death" a certain behavior or attitude?

8. What does Paul say "is coming" in verse 6? Why?

It's clear from Paul's teaching about God's wrath that one reason we should obey Christ is because God will punish sin.

- First, we should obey Christ in order to demonstrate the genuineness of our faith. Jesus says that everyone who loves him does what he commands (John 14:15). If we do not obey Jesus's commands, we do not belong to him, which means that we are facing God's wrath.

- Second, God's wrath against sin should motivate us to flee from it and to pursue righteousness because God's wrath reveals what sin really is: treason against God that deserves to be punished. Thus, meditating on God's hatred of sin should cause us to hate it too.

9. What does Paul command us to "put away," in verse 8? What does he command us not to do in verse 9? What reason does he give for why we shouldn't do these things (vv. 9–10)?

10. What does Paul say about God's attitude and actions toward us in verses 12–13? What does he tell us to do in light of these things in those verses?

In this study, we've seen that God gives us a rich variety of motivations to spur us on to grow in godliness and help others do the same:

- Our death to sin and new life in Christ (vv. 1–3).
- Our certain hope of glory with Christ (v. 4).
- The fact that God hates sin and will punish sin (v. 6).
- Our new nature in Christ (vv. 9–10).
- God's electing love for us (v. 12).
- God's forgiveness of our sins (v. 13).

11. Are any of these truths new to you? If all of them are familiar, are there ones that you haven't considered before as motivations *to grow in godliness?*

12. What are some ways you can use the truths in this passage to spur on your own and others' growth in godliness? How can you practically reshape your heart's motivations?

13. In light of this passage, what do you think are some wrong *motivations for growing in godliness? Do you personally struggle with any of these?*

14. Can you give some examples of ways that the truths we've seen in this passage have motivated your own growth in godliness or your discipleship of others? What impact have these truths already had on your discipleship?

WEEK 4
THE MEANS OF DISCIPLESHIP: FOLLOWING GODLY EXAMPLES

GETTING STARTED

Have you ever heard the phrase "Some things are better caught than taught?" It gets at the idea that some things are more easily learned by watching someone's example than through formal classroom instruction.

1. What are some things that you have learned more by imitation than by instruction?

As Christians, we certainly learn much by instruction, and we'll consider the role of teaching in our next study. But in this study, we want to consider the crucial and often overlooked truth that Christians are meant to grow through imitating godly examples.

MAIN IDEA

Learning from godly examples is a crucial aspect of Christian discipleship. This means that we should both seek out godly examples to follow and set a godly example for others.

DIGGING IN

At the end of 1 Corinthians 10, Paul concludes a long and somewhat complex discussion about meat sacrificed to idols and other issues that were troubling the Christians in Corinth. His basic point is that in all we do, we should seek the good of others. Our concern in this study is not so much the specific issue Paul addresses, but the general principles he gives us:

> [23] "All things are lawful," but not all things are helpful. "All things are lawful," but not all things build up. [24] Let no one seek his own good, but the good of his neighbor. [25] Eat whatever is sold in the meat market without raising any question on the ground of conscience. [26] For "the earth is the Lord's, and the fullness thereof." [27] If one of the unbelievers invites you to dinner and you are disposed to go, eat whatever is set before you without raising any question on the ground of conscience. [28] But if someone says to you, "This has been offered in sacrifice," then do not eat it, for the sake of the one who informed you, and for the sake of conscience— [29] I do not mean your conscience, but his. For why should my liberty be determined by someone else's conscience? [30] If I partake with thankfulness, why am I denounced because of that for which I give thanks?
>
> [31] So, whether you eat or drink, or whatever you do, do all to the glory of God. [32] Give no offense to Jews or to Greeks or to the church of God, [33] just as I try to please everyone in everything I do, not seeking my own advantage, but that of many, that they may be saved. [11:1] Be imitators of me, as I am of Christ. (1 Cor. 10:23–11:1)

1. What fault does Paul find with the saying "All things are lawful" (vv. 23–24)? What does this teach us about Paul's priorities as a Christian?

2. In verses 28–29, Paul instructs the Corinthians to accommodate themselves to the sensitivities of other people's consciences in order to not lead others into sin. What kind of attitude does this reflect?

3. What reason does Paul give for why he tries to please everyone in everything (v. 33)?

4. What does Paul tell us to do in 11:1?

5. Does it seem self-centered or proud to you for one Christian to say to another, "Imitate me, as I imitate Christ"? Why or why not?

6. Why do you think Paul tells the Corinthians to imitate his conduct, in addition to giving them instructions in writing? Why is imitating others' good examples an important aspect of discipleship?

Second Timothy 3 gives us another example of discipleship by imitation. In the first part of the chapter (vv. 1–9), Paul warns Timothy about ungodly people who will oppose the truth. Then, in verse 10, he tells Timothy how he should conduct himself in the face of this opposition:

> [10] You, however, have followed my teaching, my conduct, my aim in life, my faith, my patience, my love, my steadfastness, [11] my persecutions and sufferings that happened to me at Antioch, at Iconium, and at Lystra—which persecutions I endured; yet from them all the Lord rescued me. [12] Indeed, all who desire to live a godly life in Christ Jesus will be persecuted, [13] while evil people and impostors will go on from bad to worse, deceiving and being deceived. [14] But as for you, continue in what you have learned and have firmly believed, knowing from whom you learned it [15] and how from childhood you have been acquainted with the sacred writings, which are able to make you wise for salvation through faith in Christ Jesus. [16] All Scripture is breathed out by God and profitable for teaching, for reproof, for correction, and for training in righteousness, [17] that the man of God may be complete, equipped for every good work. (2 Tim. 3:10–17)

7. What has Timothy "followed" (vv. 10–11)? How will this help him to resist ungodly influences?

8. What does Paul say will happen to:

   a) All who desire to live a godly life in Christ Jesus (v. 12)?
   b) Evil people and impostors (v. 13)?

9. What does Paul tell Timothy to do in light of this (vv. 14–15)? Why does it matter that Timothy remembers the person "from whom [he] learned" what he firmly believes?

As we've seen in both of these passages, imitating godly examples is crucial to discipleship.

Paul instructs the Corinthians to imitate him as he imitates Christ. This means that they should humbly seek the good of others in everything they do, in order that non-Christians may come to faith in Christ and that believers may be built up in the faith. Thus, for the Corinthians—and for us—to follow Paul's example is to gear one's whole life around helping others come to Christ and grow in Christ.

And in 2 Timothy, Paul reminds Timothy that he personally knows about Paul's whole way of life: his teaching, conduct, aim in life, faith, patience, love, steadfastness, and the persecutions that he endured and from which the Lord delivered him. And, in the face of opposition from ungodly people, Paul urges Timothy to remember his way of life and to imitate it.

Imitating godly examples is crucial to discipleship, and all Christians are called to grow as disciples and to help others grow as disciples. Therefore, all Christians should both seek to imitate godly examples and to serve as godly examples for others.

10. As we've seen throughout this study, it's important for Christians to learn through imitation in addition to instruction. What are some pitfalls of learning by instruction only and not having close relationships with godly role models?

11. If learning by imitation is a large part of discipleship, why is being involved in a healthy church crucial for the Christian life?

12. Within the life of the church, what are some practical steps which the call to imitate godly examples requires you to take?

13. As a Christian, you have the responsibility—and the joyful opportunity—to set a godly example for others to follow. How should that impact the way you live your day-to-day life? What are some practical steps you can take to personally model godliness for others?

WEEK 5
THE MEANS OF DISCIPLESHIP: TEACHING ONE ANOTHER

GETTING STARTED

1. *Think about some of the Christians who have taught you the most. What makes them good teachers?*

MAIN IDEA

All Christians are called to speak the truth in love to one another in order to help each other grow up in godliness. One of the chief means by which we grow as disciples is through personal relationships in which we bring the truths of the gospel to bear on the details of life.

DIGGING IN

In Romans 15:14–16, Paul writes,

> [14] I myself am satisfied about you, my brothers, that you yourselves are full of goodness, filled with all knowledge and able to instruct one another. [15] But on some points I have written to you very boldly by way of reminder, because of the grace given me by God [16] to be a minister of Christ Jesus to the Gentiles in the priestly service of the gospel of God, so that the offering of the Gentiles may be acceptable, sanctified by the Holy Spirit.

1. *Do you think Paul would write verse 14 about your church? Why or why not?*

2. *Why do you think Paul tells the Romans that he is confident that they are able to instruct one another (v. 14)? What do you think Paul expects them to do in response?*

GROWING ONE ANOTHER

3. Do you think of yourself as able to instruct others, and other church members as able to instruct you? Why or why not?

As we've seen in Romans 15:14, it's clear that Paul expected all church members to instruct each other. In Ephesians 4, Paul gives more explicit instruction on the subject and discusses how the whole church grows to maturity:

> [11] And he gave the apostles, the prophets, the evangelists, the shepherds and teachers, [12] to equip the saints for the work of ministry, for building up the body of Christ, [13] until we all attain to the unity of the faith and of the knowledge of the Son of God, to mature manhood, to the measure of the stature of the fullness of Christ, [14] so that we may no longer be children, tossed to and fro by the waves and carried about by every wind of doctrine, by human cunning, by craftiness in deceitful schemes. [15] Rather, speaking the truth in love, we are to grow up in every way into him who is the head, into Christ, [16] from whom the whole body, joined and held together by every joint with which it is equipped, when each part is working properly, makes the body grow so that it builds itself up in love. (Eph. 4:11–16)

4. According to this passage, what is a pastor's responsibility (vv. 11–12)? How is this different from how we often think about "ministry"?

5. Who does Paul say is to attain to the unity of the faith and to the measure of the fullness of Christ? (v. 13)

6. According to verse 15, by what means are we to grow up into Christ?

7. Based on this entire passage, whom does Paul have in mind when he talks about "speaking the truth in love" (v. 15)?

8. Read verse 16. In this verse Paul teaches that the body of Christ grows as every single part "is working properly." What are some practical ways that you can help to ensure that other church members are contributing to the body's growth?

9. How would you describe your role and responsibilities as a church member in light of this passage? What should you be consistently striving to do in the church?

In Titus 2, we see an example of the kind of "speaking the truth in love" that Paul commands in Ephesians 4. In this chapter Paul tells Titus,

> [1] But as for you, teach what accords with sound doctrine. [2] Older men are to be sober-minded, dignified, self-controlled, sound in faith, in love, and in steadfastness. [3] Older women likewise are to be reverent in behavior, not slanderers or slaves to much wine. They are to teach what is good, [4] and so train the young women to love their husbands and children, [5] to be self-controlled, pure, working at home, kind, and submissive to their own husbands, that the word of God may not be reviled. [6] Likewise, urge the younger men to be self-controlled. [7] Show yourself in all respects to be a model of good works, and in your teaching show integrity, dignity, [8] and sound speech that cannot be condemned, so that an opponent may be put to shame, having nothing evil to say about us. (Titus 2:1–8)

10. What does Paul tell Titus to exhort the older women to do with respect to their own personal conduct (v. 3)? What special task do they have with respect to the younger women (vv. 4–5)?

11. What are some concrete ways women in your church can carry out Paul's instructions?

12. Based on the rest of Scripture, what do you think Paul would exhort older men to teach to younger men? Cite specific passages.

13. Think about all the passages we've looked at in this study. How would you summarize their teaching about the ways we grow in godliness?

14. What are some practical ways you can begin speaking the truth in love into other believers' lives? For starters, think about opportunities you already have, such as:

a) Weekly church gatherings
b) Small groups
c) Church members who may live nearby

WEEK 6
THE ENEMY OF
DISCIPLESHIP:
INDWELLING SIN

GETTING STARTED

1. As you seek to grow as a Christian and help others grow as Christians, what are some of the main challenges you face? How do you respond to them?

MAIN IDEA

The sin that still dwells within us and within others opposes our discipleship every step of the way, but by God's grace we can overcome it.

DIGGING IN

In Romans 7:1–12, Paul says that even though God's law is good, it brings death to sinful people because it provokes our sinful natures to act out against it. Then, in verses 13 through 25, he discusses how, even though we Christians have been given new life by the Spirit and are no longer under sin's dominion, sin still dwells in us and opposes our efforts to grow in Christ.

> [13] Did that which is good, then, bring death to me? By no means! It was sin, producing death in me through what is good, in order that sin might be shown to be sin, and through the commandment might become sinful beyond measure. [14] For we know that the law is spiritual, but I am of the flesh, sold under sin. [15] For I do not understand my own actions. For I do not do what I want, but I do the very thing I hate. [16] Now if I do what I do not want, I agree with the law, that it is good. [17] So now it is no longer I who do it, but sin that dwells within me. [18] For I know that nothing good dwells in me, that is, in my flesh. For I have the desire to do what is right, but not the ability to carry it out. [19] For I do not do the good I want, but the evil I do not want is

what I keep on doing. [20] Now if I do what I do not want, it is no longer I who do it, but sin that dwells within me.

[21] So I find it to be a law that when I want to do right, evil lies close at hand. [22] For I delight in the law of God, in my inner being, [23] but I see in my members another law waging war against the law of my mind and making me captive to the law of sin that dwells in my members. [24] Wretched man that I am! Who will deliver me from this body of death? [25] Thanks be to God through Jesus Christ our Lord! So then, I myself serve the law of God with my mind, but with my flesh I serve the law of sin. (Rom. 7:13–25)

1. Why doesn't Paul understand his own actions (v. 15)?

2. What does Paul conclude from the fact that he does the opposite of what he wants (v. 17)?

3. Does this mean that Paul isn't responsible for what he does? Why or why not?

4. What does Paul have? What does he lack (v. 18)?

5. What does Paul find to be a law, that is, a regular, predictable pattern (v. 21)?

6. How would you summarize Paul's struggle in your own words?

7. Can you identify with this struggle? If so, in what ways?

8. What does this passage teach us about the nature of sin? Is this different from how you typically think about sin?

9. In light of this passage's teaching, what should our attitude toward sin be? What should it not be?

10. Read Romans 8:12–13. What does Paul tell us to do to the sin that dwells within us? What are some practical means by which we can do that on a day-to-day basis?

11. As we've seen in previous studies, all of us are called to help our fellow church members grow in Christ through teaching the Word and modeling godly living for others.

What are some ways that sin can threaten discipleship in the church? What are some of the ways Scripture calls us to respond when others sin against us? Discuss the following passages:

- Matthew 18:15–20
- Romans 12:17–19
- Galatians 6:1–5
- Ephesians 4:32
- 1 Peter 4:8

12. Consider the Scripture passages we've just discussed. Which of these responses to sin do you find to be most difficult? Why? What are some things that could help you grow in this area?

WEEK 7
THE END OF DISCIPLESHIP

GETTING STARTED

A marathon may only last for four or five hours, but (so I'm told) those few hours can feel pretty long when you're in the middle of them. Not only that, but to successfully run a marathon you have to train for months on end, building up the necessary endurance and stamina.

Whether in the race itself or in training, keeping a clear eye on the finish line is essential to getting through a long, difficult task such as a marathon.

1. Think of a long, difficult task you've undertaken. What was its end goal? How did your hope of achieving that goal influence the way you worked at that task?

MAIN IDEA

At the end, God will make all believers perfect in holiness. This certain hope energizes, encourages, and sustains our efforts to grow and help others grow in holiness here and now.

DIGGING IN

In Colossians 1:24–26, Paul talks about how he rejoices in suffering for the sake of the gospel, which was formerly hidden but has now been revealed to all the saints. He goes on,

> [27] To them God chose to make known how great among the Gentiles are the riches of the glory of this mystery, which is Christ in you, the hope of glory. [28] Him we proclaim, warning everyone and teaching everyone with all wisdom, that we may present everyone mature in Christ. [29] For this I toil, struggling with all his energy that he powerfully works within me. (Col. 1:27–29)

1. What is the mystery which has now been made known to the saints (v. 27)?

2. Whom does Paul proclaim? In what manner does Paul proclaim him (v. 28)?

3. For what purpose or goal does Paul proclaim Christ (v. 28)?

4. How hard does Paul work to present everyone mature in Christ (v. 29)?

When Paul talks about presenting everyone mature in Christ, he has the last day in mind. On that day, all those who believe in Christ will stand before God perfected in righteousness. In this life we never attain perfection. As we considered in our last study, sin still dwells within all of us as long as we live. But on the last day we will be presented complete in Christ.

And notice that this doesn't lead Paul to kick back and say, "Well, you'll be made perfect on the last day, so we don't really need to worry about it right now." Instead he does exactly the opposite! Since he knows that believers will be made perfect on the last day, he toils and struggles with all the energy God works within him.

5. What does this teach us about what discipleship demands of us, both as we seek to grow in Christ and as we seek to help others grow in Christ?

6. If we are to work to present every person mature in Christ, why are both "warning" and "teaching" important? What are some things we need to warn and teach each other about?

What John says in 1 John 3 nicely complements what Paul tells us about the goal and aim of his ministry. John writes,

> [1] See what kind of love the Father has given to us, that we should be called children of God; and so we are. The reason why the world does not know us is that it did not know him. [2] Beloved, we are God's children now, and what we will be has not yet appeared; but we know that when he appears we shall be like him, because we shall see him

as he is. ³ And everyone who thus hopes in him purifies himself as he is pure. (1 John 3:1–3)

7. *What has God done to us to demonstrate his love for us (v. 1)?*

8. *Why doesn't the world know us? Why should this be a comfort and encouragement to us (v. 1)?*

9. *What will happen to us when Christ appears? Why (v. 2)?*

10. *What does everyone who hopes in Christ do because of this hope (v. 3)?*

11. *In light of this passage and the prior one, how would you respond to someone who said, "If God is going to purify us from sin in the end, why do we need to bother about that now? Can't we just keep on living however we want, since God is going to perfect us in the end?"*

12. *What are some causes for discouragement in the discipleship process? How does this passage give encouragement and strengthen our hope as we persevere in growing in Christ and helping others grow in Christ?*

13. *What are some specific ways you can grow as a disciple, and help others grow as disciples, by bringing the hope of glory to bear on the stuff of our daily lives?*

TEACHER'S NOTES FOR WEEK 1

DIGGING IN

1. Paul says that he *is not yet* perfect and that he *has not yet* attained to the resurrection (vv. 12–13).

2. If this is how the apostle Paul viewed himself, we should also view ourselves as not yet perfect and recognize that we all need to grow as Christians.

3. The reason Paul gives for why he presses on to obtain a deeper knowledge of Christ is that Christ has already made Paul his own (v. 12).

4. This teaches us that the basis and motivation for our growth as Christians is that we already belong to Christ. Paul wanted to lay hold of the knowledge of Christ because Christ had already taken hold of him. Because we've been saved by Christ, we want to know him more. Because he's forgiven our sins, we want to fight against them. What Christ has already done for us motivates us to pursue greater and greater holiness.

5. Paul says that the one thing he *does* is, "forgetting what lies behind and straining forward to what lies ahead, I press on toward the goal for the prize of the upward call of God in Christ Jesus" (Phil. 3:13–14).

6. In verses 13–14, Paul uses the imagery of an athlete running a race. This imagery teaches us that, just as athletes devote 100 percent of their energy and strength to their competition, so we also should devote serious, disciplined, energetic effort to growing as Christians.

7. In verse 17, Paul tells us to imitate him and all those who follow his example. Practically, this means that we should imitate those Christians who most faithfully live according to God's Word. Specifically, Scripture tells us to imitate our churches' leaders (Heb. 13:7).

8. That Paul instructs us to imitate his and others' example teaches us that we are to grow through imitation. That is, we are to follow others' godly examples by observing their ways of life, developing relationships with them, and imitating the ways in which they obey Jesus.

9. The threat Paul mentions to our faithfully following his and others' godly examples is that there are many false teachers who promote sin by their teaching and by their lives (vv. 18–19). This threat makes it especially important for us to follow godly examples because it is difficult to successfully resist false teachers on our own. Following in the footsteps of mature,

seasoned Christians helps us to stay on track in the faith and not be misled by false teachers.

10. In verses 20 through 21, Paul says that Christians:

- Are citizens of heaven (v. 20)
- Eagerly await the coming of our Savior, the Lord Jesus Christ (v. 20)
- Will be transformed by Christ at his coming, so that our bodies will be like his glorious body (v. 21)

That we are citizens of heaven means that we have an eternal inheritance waiting for us. As such, we should live in a way that anticipates that reality. That Christ is coming back means he will one day right every wrong and we will share in his glorious, eternal kingdom. Because our salvation will one day be made complete, we should have confidence in God's gracious work in our lives now. All of these aspects of our future hope should stir us up to fight sin and pursue holiness in the present, because we are sure of the glorious future that awaits us.

11–12. Answers will vary.

13. A person who truly fears God and not other people is, by definition, humble. And it's such a person who will, from time to time, present himself or herself as an example to be followed, not caring if other people regard this as pride.

14–15. Answers will vary.

TEACHER'S NOTES FOR WEEK 2

DIGGING IN

1. Based on what we see in these passages, following Jesus means:

- Obeying Jesus (Matt. 4:19–20)
- Denying ourselves (Matt. 16:24)
- Taking up the cross; that is, being willing to follow Jesus even unto death (Matt. 16:24)
- Serving Jesus (John 12:25–26)

2. Following Jesus does not necessarily mean that we need to leave our jobs and other responsibilities, as the first disciples did (see 1 Cor. 7:17–24). In fact, following Jesus means that we are to be responsible and faithful in whatever calling and responsibilities the Lord has given us (see, for example, Col. 3:18–4:1).

3. According to these passages, following Jesus is profoundly difficult. We must die to ourselves, follow him no matter the cost, and be willing to lose our lives for his sake. Yet in all this, God's grace enables us to obey Jesus and restores us when we fail.

4. Jesus says that all authority in heaven and on earth has been given to him (v. 18). This requires that we submit to him and obey all that he teaches.

5. Jesus commands his disciples to go and make more disciples. They are to do this through:

- Baptizing people who repent of their sins and trust in Christ. This implies that they are to proclaim the good news about Jesus's death and resurrection, since baptism is an identification with Jesus in his death and resurrection.
- Teaching them to obey everything Jesus commanded (vv. 19–20).

6. This passage applies to all believers today, not merely to the original eleven. The strongest reason for that is that the disciples are to teach the new disciples to obey everything Jesus commanded, which includes this

command to make disciples! So, one of the things that all disciples of Jesus are to do is seek to make more disciples of Jesus.

7. The encouragement Jesus gives us is that he will be with us to the end of the age (v. 20).

8. Answers will vary.

9. Answers will vary, but the basic idea is that this passage applies to all of us, not merely those of us who spend our lives preaching the gospel to people of another culture. All of us are called to make disciples, which means that all of us are called to share the gospel with others and to build up other Christians in the faith.

10–11. Answers will vary.

TEACHER'S NOTES FOR WEEK 3

DIGGING IN

1. In verse 1 Paul commands us to seek the things that are above. The basis on which he commands us to do this is that we have been raised with Christ. Our resurrection with Christ is one motive for our growth in the things of God.

2. This question is asking for a personal response. Hopefully, participants will say something like, "This does motivate me to grow as a Christian, because it reminds me that God is powerfully at work in my life. It reminds me that while before my conversion I was spiritually dead, now I'm alive to God. I love his Word. I want to obey him. I'm a new person. And it reminds me that the same power that raised Jesus from the dead is also at work in me, now."

3. Being motivated by the fact that we've died to sin and been raised with Christ is different from a "just do it" approach to discipleship (in which we obey out of a bare sense of obligation) because it starts with what God has already done for us, and in us, in Christ. Following Paul's pattern of motivation in this passage means that in order to grow as disciples, we remind ourselves of God's gracious work in the gospel. This means that our efforts are a thankful, trusting response to God's grace. And it means that we are reminded that God's power is at work within us, not merely our own efforts, which is a tremendous encouragement to keep striving for growth.

4. In verse 2 Paul commands us to set our minds on the things that are above (which is basically a restatement of his command from verse 1). The grounds on which Paul commands us to do this are that we've died (at our conversion we died to the power of sin), our life is hidden with Christ in God, and that when Christ comes we will be glorified with him.

5. Answers will vary, but here are some examples:

- Since I've died to sin, death no longer has power over me. Because I'm alive in Christ, I'm able now to obey God.
- Since I've died to my old self, I'm a new person in Christ. I've broken with sin and with my old ways. I'm no longer who I once was. So I should live like it!

- Since I've died to the world, I'm no longer under its power. I don't have to seek the world's approval or be afraid of its rejection. Christ is my Lord, and I must submit to him.

6. Answers will vary, but the basic idea is this: that our hope of future glory with Christ is certain and secure helps us to endure trials and hardships now. It reminds us that we won't have to battle sin forever. It encourages us because we have unending joy with Christ ahead of us in eternity. And all of these things put wind in our sails. They all spur us on to live now more like we will live in eternity.

7. In verse 5, Paul commands us to put to death what is earthly in us, namely, sexual immorality, impurity, passion, evil desire, and covetousness, which is idolatry. To put these actions and desires to death means that we deliberately, consistently oppose those sins in our lives. We don't feed them or nurture them. We don't indulge them or secretly enjoy them. Instead, we do everything we can to stamp them out of existence. We pray for grace to overcome them. We study Scripture in order to wield it against them. We confess them to God and other Christians, and we ask others for help in overcoming them. And so on.

8. In verse 6 Paul says that the wrath of God is coming. Why? Because of the sins he mentioned in verse 5 ("on account of these").

9. In verse 8, Paul commands us to "put away" anger, wrath, malice, slander, and obscene talk. In verse 9 he tells us not to lie to one another. And the reason he gives for these commands in verses 9 and 10 is that we have put off "the old self" and we have put on "the new self, which is being renewed in knowledge after the image of its creator." Paul is referring to our conversion, at which time we shed our old, sinful nature and put on a new nature that is alive to God and indwelt by the Spirit.

10. In verses 12–13 Paul says that God loves us, has chosen us, has made us holy, and has forgiven our sins. In light of these things, Paul tells us to "put on" compassionate hearts, kindness, humility, meekness, and patience, to bear with one another, and to forgive each other.

11. Answers will vary.

12. Answers will vary, but they include:

- Studying these things in Scripture
- Meditating on these things in Scripture
- Praying through these things and applying them to specific struggles with sin

- Personally reminding others of these truths from Scripture to encourage them
- And so on . . .

13. Answers will vary, but wrong motivations for discipleship include:

   - Trying to earn our salvation. We are saved by grace alone, through faith alone, in Christ alone. Jesus has earned salvation for us.
   - Trying to win God's love and acceptance. If we're Christians, God already loves us. He has already chosen us (vv. 12–13). He already has accepted us in Christ. We should be motivated to obey God because he loves us and accepts us, not in order to gain those things.
   - Trying to please or impress other people. We should be supremely concerned with what God thinks. We should hate sin because he hates it (v. 6) and love righteousness because we love God, who is righteous. We shouldn't try to grow in godliness in order to seem more spiritual in the eyes of other people but in order to truly become more spiritual in God's sight.

14. Answers will vary.

TEACHER'S NOTES FOR WEEK 4

DIGGING IN

1. The fault Paul finds with the saying "all things are lawful" (vv. 23–24) is that not all things are helpful and not all things build others up. Thus, Paul says that instead of being concerned to obtain the maximum degree of freedom for ourselves, we should seek the good of our neighbor and do what will build up him or her. This teaches us that Paul's fundamental priority as a Christian was to do what would spiritually build up others.

2. Paul's instructions to the Corinthians to accommodate themselves to the sensitivities of other people's consciences in order to not lead them into sin (v. 29) reflects an attitude of dying to self, considering others more important than one's self, and being willing to make sacrifices so that others would be spiritually built up.

3. The reason Paul gives for why he tries to please everyone in everything is so that others may be saved (v. 33).

4. In 1 Corinthians 11:1, Paul tells us to imitate him as he imitates Christ.

5. Answers will vary. Some people may find it prideful or offensive for one Christian to set himself up as an example for another. If that's the case, one could graciously respond that first, Paul is only instructing others to imitate him insofar as he imitates Christ. We are not to absolutely follow another Christian in every way, since we all stumble in many ways (James 3:2). Jesus is our ultimate standard, model, and example, and we are to follow other Christians insofar as they follow him. Second, it's not necessarily prideful to attempt to model godliness for others, since as Christians, we recognize that any good in us comes from God, not ourselves (1 Cor. 4:7). Finally, it's clear from this very text that Paul was not motivated by anything selfish or self-serving. Rather, his whole desire was to do others good spiritually, to build them up in Christ.

6. It seems that Paul tells the Corinthians to imitate his conduct, in addition to giving them written instruction, because there's a way that someone's example makes a special impact on us. This is true of bad examples as well as of good ones (see 1 Cor. 15:33)! Whether we think of our parents, a teacher, a pastor, a friend, or any other kind of mentor, we know that people's personal examples make a deep, lasting imprint on our hearts and minds. When you see someone living out the truth, it challenges and inspires you

to do the same. Not only that, but as you see someone's example of living in light of the gospel in every area of life, you gain valuable practical wisdom about how to live as a Christian. Thus, imitating godly examples is important in discipleship because it gives us footsteps in which to follow. It helps to practically teach us *how* to live.

7. Timothy has "followed" Paul's whole way of life, including his teaching, conduct, aim in life, faith, patience, love, steadfastness, and the persecutions, which he endured and from which the Lord delivered him (vv. 10–11). This will help him resist ungodly influences because with Paul's godly character vividly before his eyes, he will be better enabled to resist ungodly influences. Having personally seen and known Paul's way of life, he will be able to imitate Paul.

8. Paul says that

   a) All who desire to live a godly life in Christ Jesus will be persecuted (v. 12).
   b) Evil people and impostors will go from bad to worse, deceiving and being deceived (v. 13).

9. In light of this, Paul tells Timothy to continue in what he has learned and believed, since he knows whom he has learned it from, and since he knows the Scriptures (vv. 14–15). It matters that Timothy remembers the person "from whom he learned" what he firmly believes because Paul's example of faithfulness through persecution will enable him to be faithful as well.

10–13. Answers will vary.

TEACHER'S NOTES FOR WEEK 5

DIGGING IN

1. Answers will vary. Hopefully, participants will recognize that all Christians, not merely those in the Roman church to whom Paul wrote, are able to instruct one another because we all have God's Spirit within us.

2. It seems that Paul tells the Romans that he is confident that they are able to instruct one another:

- To remind them that, even though he was exhorting them firmly, it was not because he thought they were lacking in knowledge or ability
- In order to stir them up to do that very thing!

In other words, by reminding them that he was convinced they were able to teach each other, Paul was conveying his expectation that everyone in the church *would* teach each other.

3. Answers will vary.

4. According to this passage, a pastor's responsibility is to equip the saints for the work of ministry (vv. 11–12). This is different from how we often think of ministry in that we typically think that pastors are the ones who *do* ministry, and the rest of us just passively receive their teaching. But Paul teaches that the purpose of pastors' work is to equip *all of us* to do the work of building up the body of Christ.

5. Paul says that *we all*—that is, every single believer in Christ—are to attain to the unity of the faith and to the measure of the fullness of Christ (v. 13).

6. According to verse 15, the means by which we are to grow up into Christ is through speaking the truth in love to one another.

7. Based on this entire passage, when Paul talks about "speaking the truth in love" he has *all of us* in mind. That is, Paul exhorts every single one of us to speak truth in love to our fellow church members so that we would all grow to maturity in Christ.

8. Answers will vary.

9. The basic idea is that each church member should seek to build up others in godliness through teaching God's Word to them and applying it to their

lives. For most of us, this will take place privately, in personal relationships or perhaps in small groups. For others, it will involve teaching in larger and more public settings. But the point is that every Christian should actively seek to help others grow in conformity to Christ through speaking truth in love to them.

10. Paul tells Titus to exhort the older women to be reverent, not be slanderers, and not be slaves to much wine (v. 3). The special task he gives them with respect to the younger women is that they are to teach them "what is good, and so train the young women to love their husbands and children, to be self-controlled, pure, working at home, kind, and submissive to their own husbands, that the word of God may not be reviled" (vv. 4–5). In other words, the older women are to disciple the younger women by teaching them to faithfully carry out the unique responsibilities God has entrusted to them as women.

11. Answers will vary.

12. Answers will vary, but should include:

- Men who are husbands are to love their wives as Christ loves the church (Eph. 5:25–32).
- Men who are fathers are to raise their children in the discipline and nurture of the Lord (Eph. 6:4) and are not to provoke them to discouragement (Col. 3:21).
- Men are to work diligently in order to provide for their families' material needs (1 Tim. 5:8).

13. A good summary of these passages' teaching about the way we are to grow in godliness would be along these lines: We are to grow in godliness through teaching and being taught by fellow believers. All of us should continually be speaking God's Word into each other's' lives so that we may all grow up in godliness.

14. Answers will vary.

TEACHER'S NOTES FOR WEEK 6

DIGGING IN

1. Paul doesn't understand his own actions because he doesn't do the thing he wants—that is, to obey God's Word. Instead, he does the very thing he hates, namely, sin (v. 15).

2. Paul concludes from the fact that he does the opposite of what he wants that it is not him doing this, but sin that dwells within him (v. 17).

3. This does *not* mean that Paul isn't responsible for what he does. When Paul says that it is no longer him acting, but sin that dwells within him, he does not mean that he is not going to be held morally accountable for his actions. After all, it's still *him* acting, and Paul clearly states that all believers will give an account to God (Rom. 14:10–12). His point in this passage is simply that sin dwells within him as an active, hostile force, keeping him from doing the things which his godly, renewed, Spirit-given nature wants to do.

4. Paul has the desire to do what is good, but he lacks the ability to carry it out (v. 18).

5. Paul finds it to be a law (a regular, predictable pattern) that when he wants to do right, evil lies close at hand (v. 21).

6. A good summary of this passage would be something like this: As someone who has been born again by the Holy Spirit and given a new nature by God, Paul longs to do what pleases God at all times. Yet because sin still dwells in him, he often finds himself unable to do the good he wants to do, and instead he does the evil he doesn't want to do. Thus Paul finds sin to be a powerful, hostile, active enemy that lives inside of him, trying to take his will captive to do evil. This causes Paul to cry out to Jesus Christ for deliverance, and Paul is confident that he will be delivered from sin by Christ.

7. Answers will vary, but every Christian should be able to identify with this struggle in one way or another, because all true Christians have been given a new nature by God that delights to do his will, and yet all of us still have sin dwelling within us which entices us to do evil.

8. This passage teaches us that sin is a pervasive, powerful, active force that still lives in us as believers. Often, we think about sin only in terms of specific sins we commit. This passage teaches us to look deeper and realize that

sin is actually an enemy that lives within us, which we must actively resist with all our might.

9. In light of this passage's teaching, our attitude toward sin should be one of active, alert, wary opposition. We should recognize that sin is out to enslave our wills, and we must be on our guard against it. A wrong attitude toward sin could include complacency, apathy, indulgence, minimizing its importance, underestimating its danger, and more.

10. In Romans 8:12–13, Paul tells us to put to death by the Spirit the sin that dwells within us. Practical means by which we can do this on a day-to-day basis include:

- Confessing our sin to God and asking for forgiveness
- Confessing to God that we hate our sin and asking him for gracious enablement to overcome it
- Reading, studying, meditating on, and memorizing Scripture, so that it saturates our hearts and minds
- Regularly and wholeheartedly participating in the church's corporate worship, so that our hearts and minds are shaped by worshiping God, praying with God's people, and especially hearing God's Word preached
- Seeking counsel and accountability from fellow believers
- Confessing sins to trusted friends and asking for their help in overcoming them
- And more . . .

11. There are countless ways that sin can threaten discipleship in the church, including:

- Causing personal offense to others
- Unintentionally discouraging others through careless words
- Threatening the church's unity
- And many more . . .

Some of the ways Scripture calls us to respond when others sin against us include:

- Privately confronting someone who sins against us in order to secure their repentance (Matt. 18:15–20).
- Taking along another individual or two if the person doesn't repent the first time (Matt. 18:15–20).

- Bringing the matter before the whole church if the person still does not repent (Matt. 18:15–20).
- Not retaliating or seeking revenge when someone wrongs us, but rather overcoming evil with good (Rom. 12:17–19).
- Gently restoring someone who is caught in sin, helping to put them on the right path again (Gal. 6:1–5).
- Forgiving others as we've been forgiven (Eph. 4:32).
- Covering over sin through love (1 Pet. 4:8). Rather than responding in kind, we should smother sin like we'd smother a fire under a wet blanket.

12. Answers will vary.

TEACHER'S NOTES FOR WEEK 7

DIGGING IN

1. The mystery which has now been made known to the saints is "Christ in you, the hope of glory" (Col. 1:27). Christ's death and resurrection bring about a whole new reality for us who believe—a reality that was foreshadowed, but not clearly disclosed, in the Old Testament. Now, Christ lives in us, which is a tangible foretaste of the glory that certainly awaits us.

2. Paul proclaims Christ (v. 28). The manner in which Paul proclaims Christ is by warning and teaching everyone in all wisdom (v. 28).

3. Paul proclaims Christ, warning and teaching everyone in all wisdom, *in order to* present everyone mature in Christ (v. 28). That is, Paul labors to bring believers to full maturity in Christ in preparation for the last day, on which God will perfect the work of sanctification which he began in this life.

4. In order to present everyone mature in Christ, Paul says that he toils, struggling with all the energy that God powerfully works within him (v. 29). In other words, Paul works *hard*—as hard as he can. Paul viewed the task of discipling Christians as demanding all that he had to give, and he gave himself wholly to it.

5. This teaches us that discipleship demands constant, diligent, earnest effort. It's not easy! None of us becomes more holy automatically. It takes grace-driven effort for us to grow in overcoming sin and in holy living. And it takes grace-driven effort for us to help others do the same.

6. If we are to work to present every person mature in Christ, "warning" is important because, as we considered last week, sin is a deadly enemy that lurks within us and seeks to take us captive to do evil. The book of Hebrews says that sin hardens our hearts and tries to cause us to fall away from the living God (Heb. 3:12–13). Thus we need to be warned about sin's power, deceitfulness, and devastating consequences. And teaching is important because personal transformation comes about as our minds are renewed by God's Word (Rom. 12:1–2).

Regarding what some things are that we need to warn and teach each other about, there is a multitude of good answers.

7. What God has done to us to demonstrate his love for us is that he has made us his children (v. 1).

8. The world doesn't know us because it did not know Jesus (v. 2). That is, it did not recognize him and accept him as the Son of God. This should be a comfort and encouragement to us because when the world rejects and persecutes us, we know that they did the same to Jesus, and we should expect to be treated the same way he was. Jesus has experienced this before us, and he is a sympathetic helper and comforter for us when we undergo trials.

9. When Christ appears, we will be like him, because we will see him as he is (v. 2). This doesn't mean that we will be divine like him, but we will be made perfect in holiness like him.

10. Everyone who hopes in Christ purifies himself, just as he is pure, because of this hope (v. 3).

11. In light of this passage, an appropriate answer would be something like, "As Christians, we are counted righteous in God's sight by faith alone, which motivates us to actually live a righteous life, since we know we are accepted by God. Similarly, the certainty that we will one day be made perfect fuels and encourages our efforts to grow in holiness. Further, we know that *only* those who strive for holiness in this life will be glorified on the last day (1 Cor. 6:9–11)."

12–13. Answers will vary.

PERSONAL NOTES

PERSONAL NOTES

9Marks

Building Healthy Churches

9Marks exists to equip church leaders with a biblical vision and practical resources for displaying God's glory to the nations through healthy churches.

To that end, we want to see churches characterized by these nine marks of health:

1 Expositional Preaching
2 Biblical Theology
3 A Biblical Understanding of the Gospel
4 A Biblical Understanding of Conversion
5 A Biblical Understanding of Evangelism
6 Biblical Church Membership
7 Biblical Church Discipline
8 Biblical Discipleship
9 Biblical Church Leadership

Find all our Crossway titles
and other resources at
www.9Marks.org

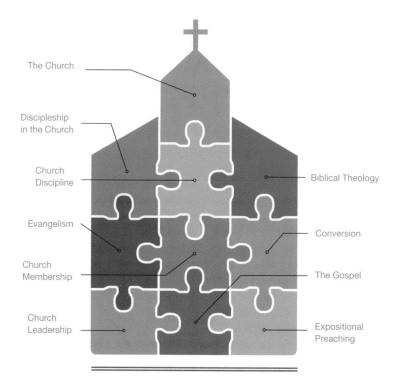

The Church

Discipleship
in the Church

Church
Discipline

Evangelism

Church
Membership

Church
Leadership

Biblical Theology

Conversion

The Gospel

Expositional
Preaching

Be sure to check out the rest of the
**9MARKS HEALTHY CHURCH
STUDY GUIDE SERIES**

This series covers the nine distinctives
of a healthy church as originally laid out
in *Nine Marks of a Healthy Church* by
Mark Dever. Each book explores the
biblical foundations of key aspects of
the church, helping Christians to live
out those realities as members of a
local body. A perfect resource for use in
Sunday school, church-wide studies, or
small group contexts.